HUMAN BODY BOOK
INTRODUCTION TO THE CIRCULATORY SYSTEM
Children's Anatomy & Physiology Edition

SPEEDY
PUBLISHING

Speedy Publishing LLC
40 E. Main St. #1156
Newark, DE 19711
www.speedypublishing.com

Copyright 2015

The heart is one of the only muscles that works in your body without you having to think about it.

The circulatory system
is also called the
cardiovascular system
or the vascular system.

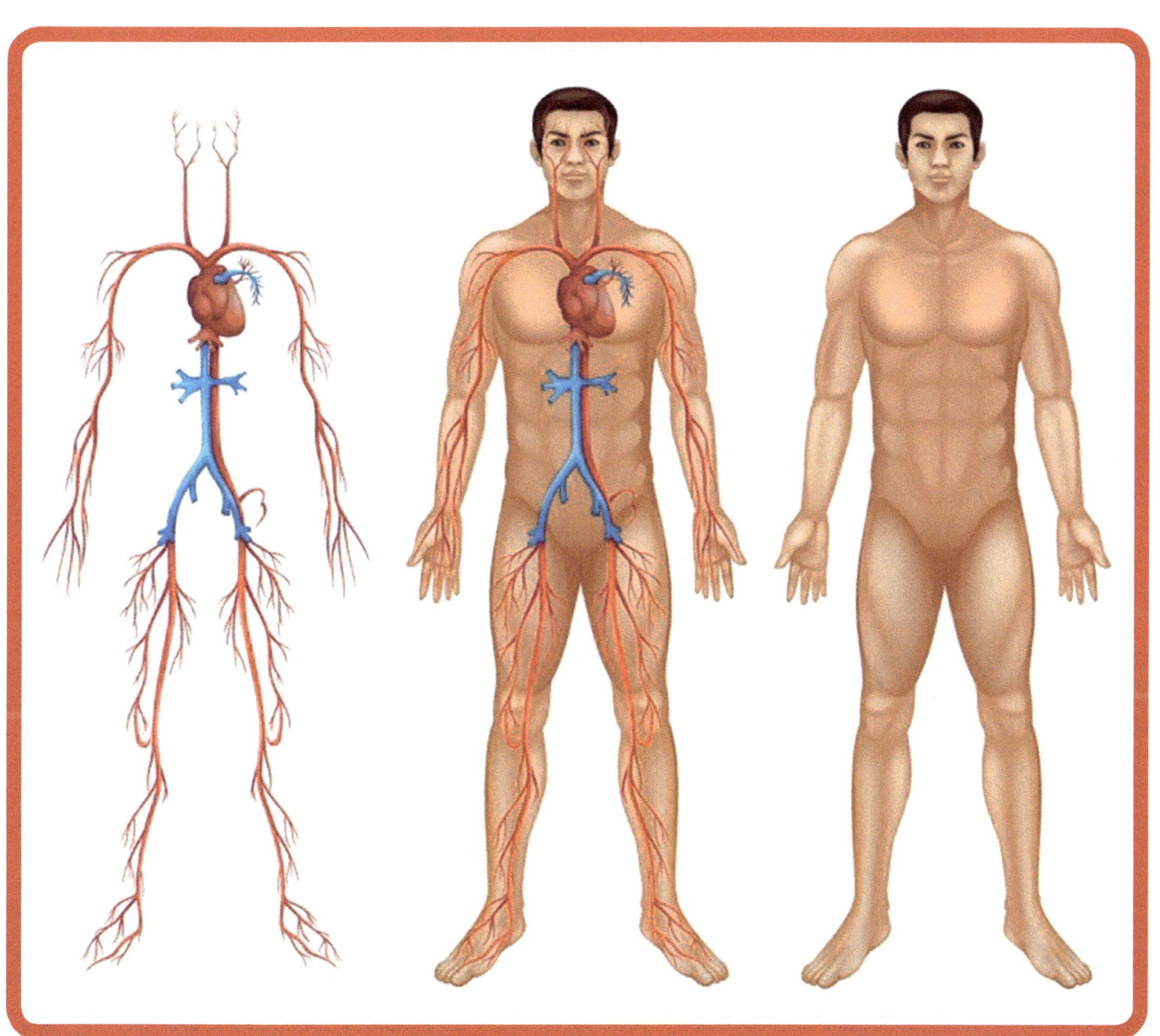

The circulatory system
is a vast network of
organs and vessels
that is responsible
for the flow of blood,
nutrients, hormones,
oxygen and other gases
to and from cells.

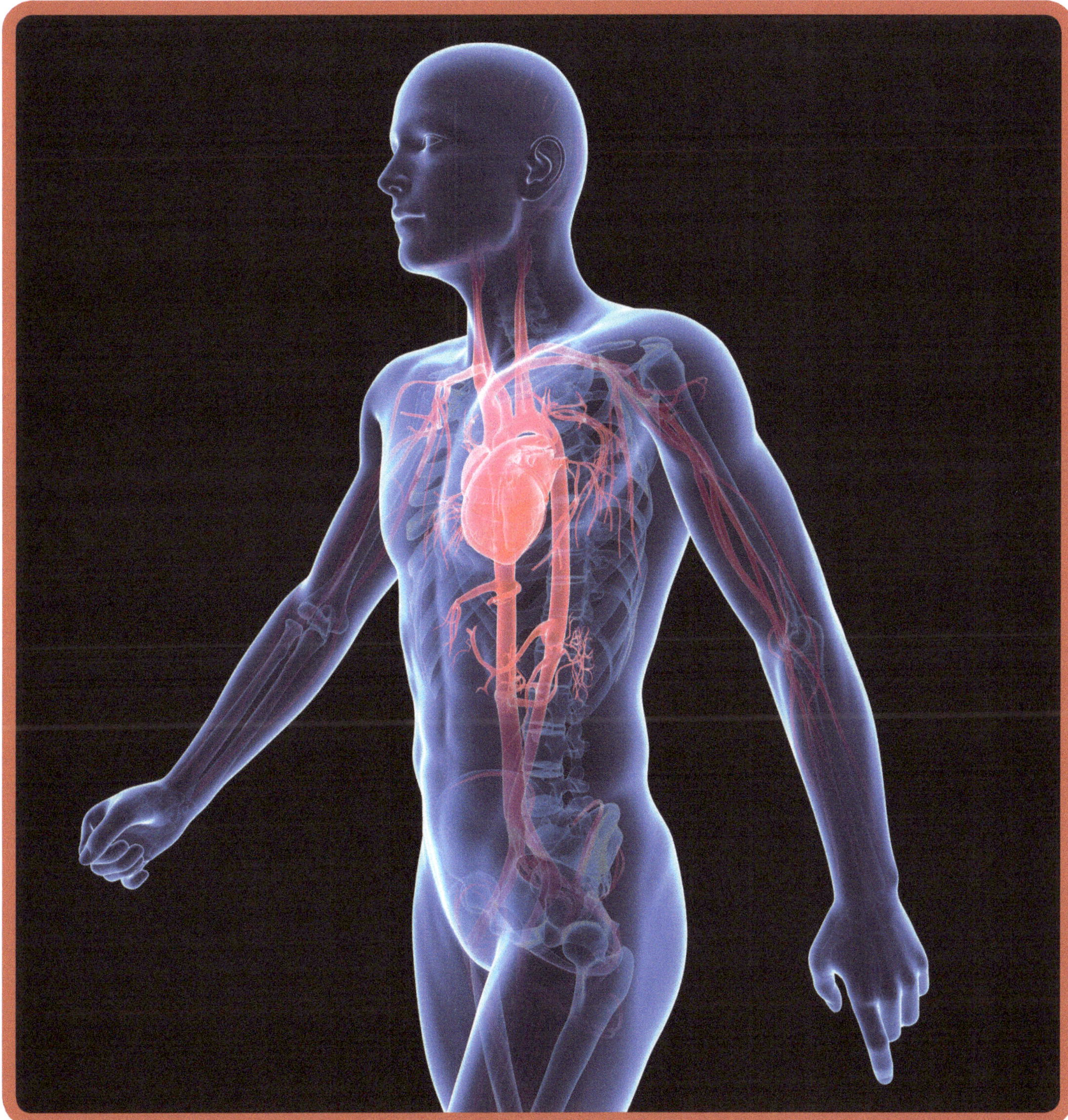

The circulatory system
is centred on the heart,
a muscular organ that
rhythmically pumps
blood around a complex
network of blood vessels
extending to every
part of the body.

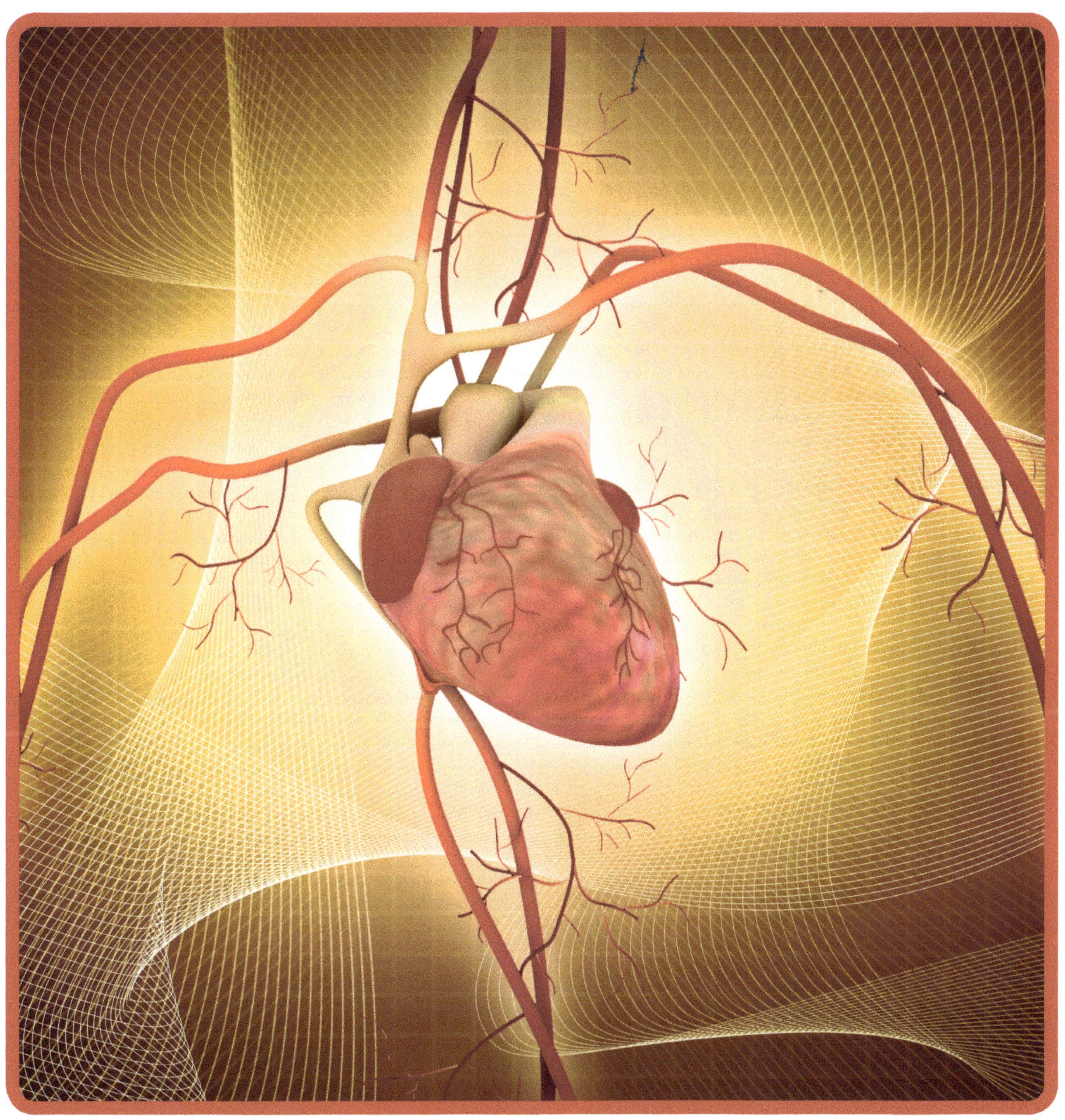

Blood carries the oxygen and nutrients needed to fuel the activities of the body's tissues and organs.

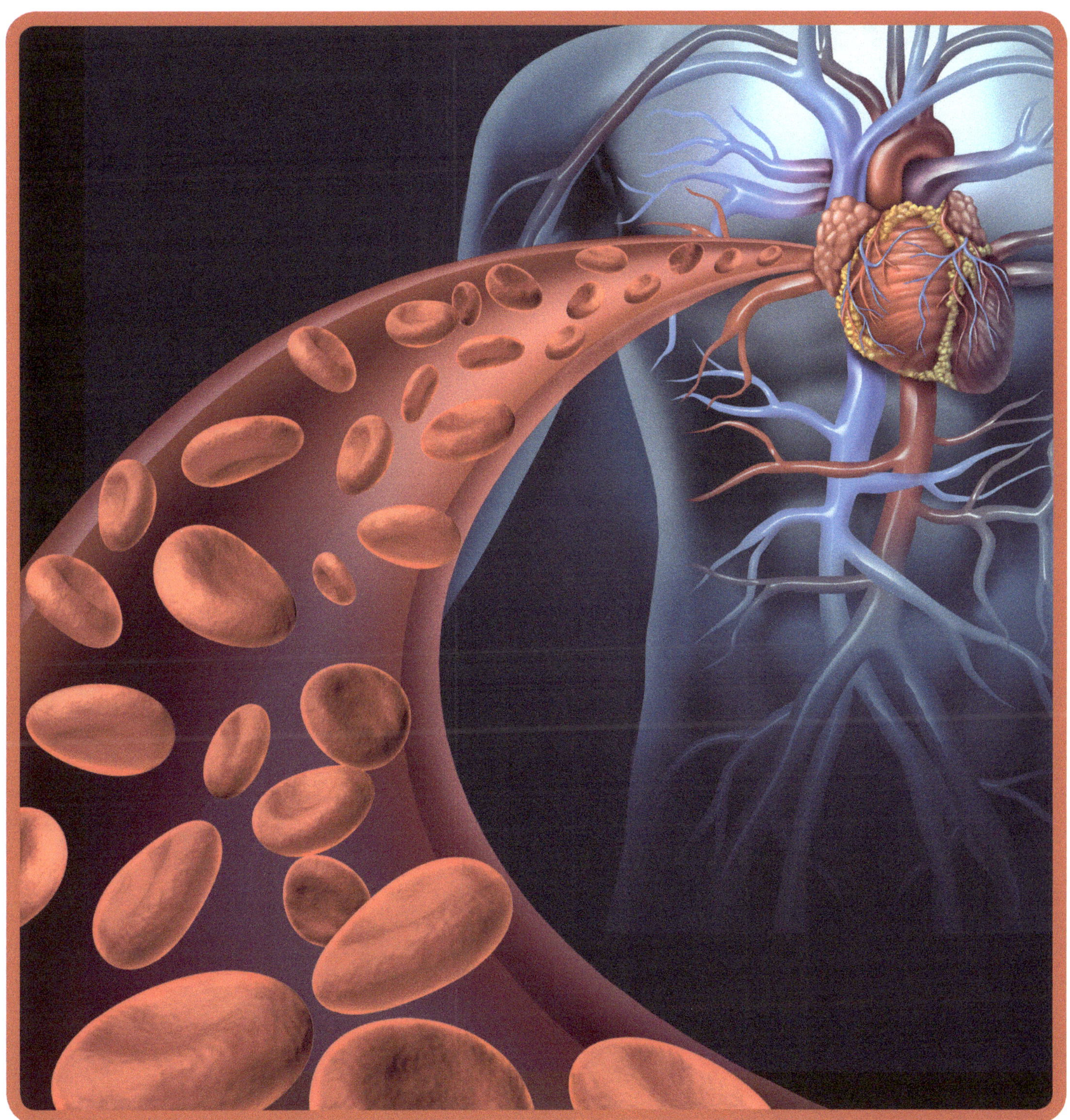

Capillaries are tiny,
averaging about 8
microns in diameter,
or about a tenth
of the diameter of
a human hair.

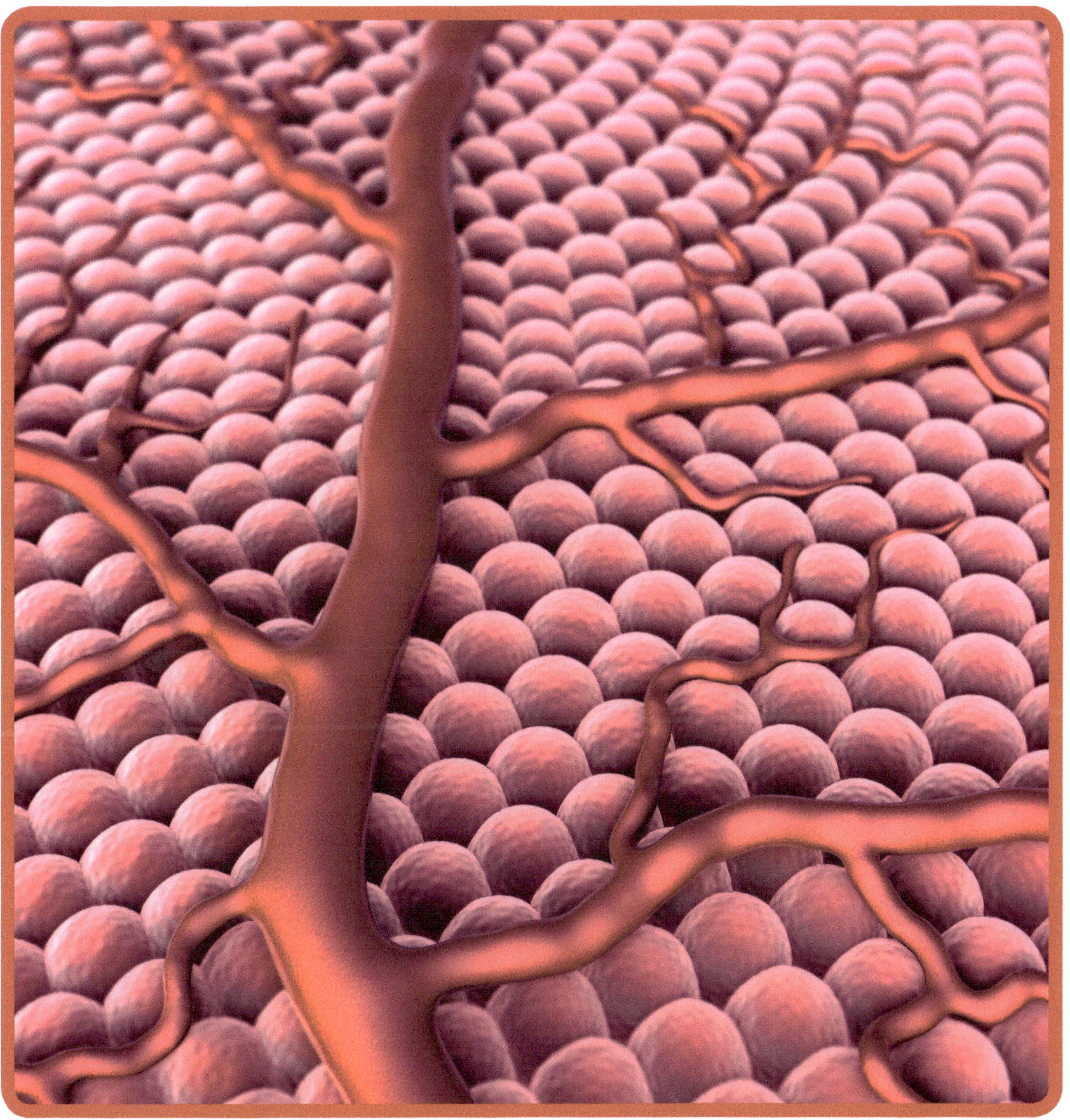

Red blood cells are about the same size as the capillaries through which they travel, so these cells must move in single-file lines.

Blood consists of plasma, red blood cells, white blood cells, and platelets.

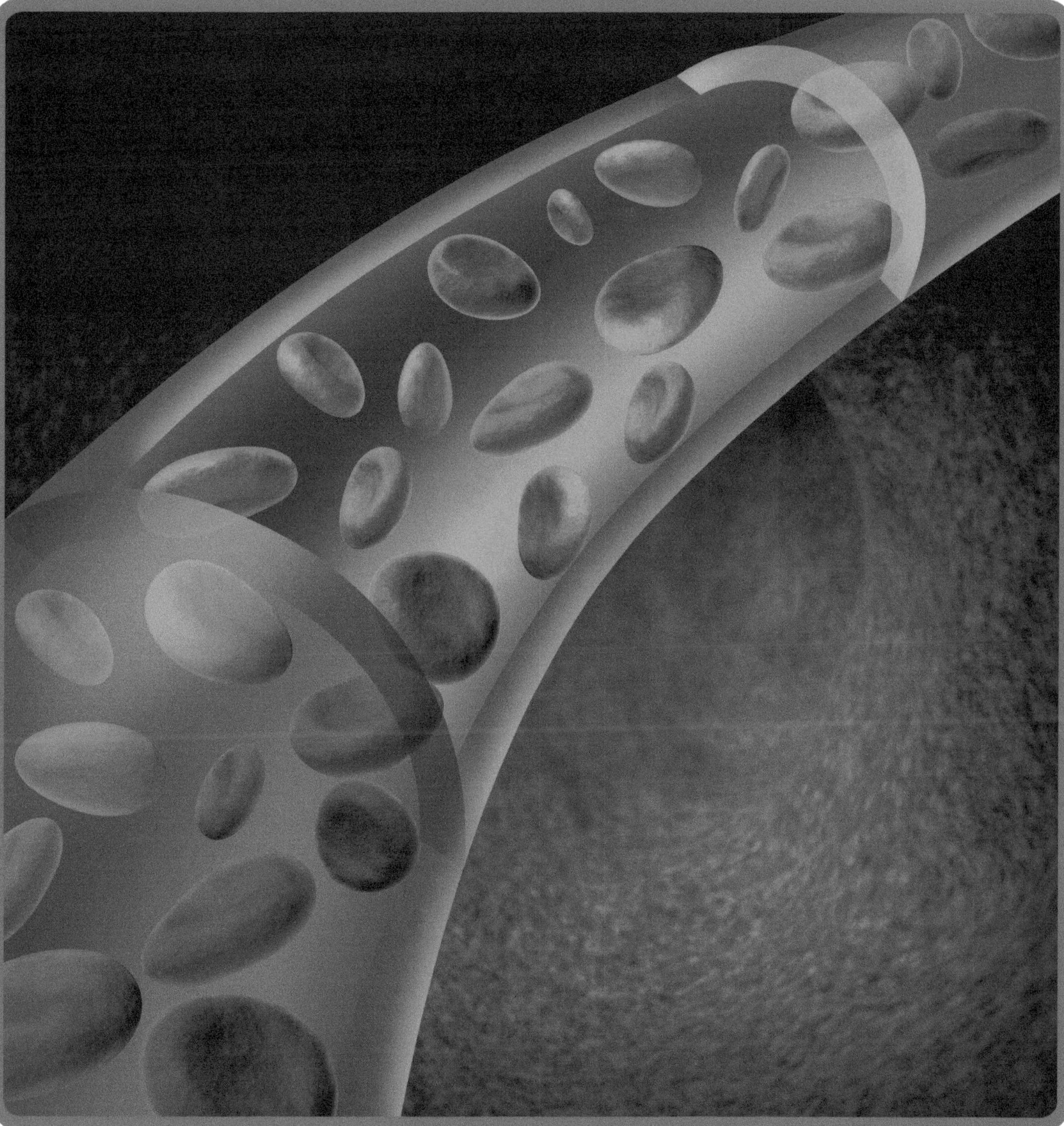

Arteries are blood vessels that carry blood away from the heart.

Arteries have a higher blood pressure than other parts of the circulatory system.

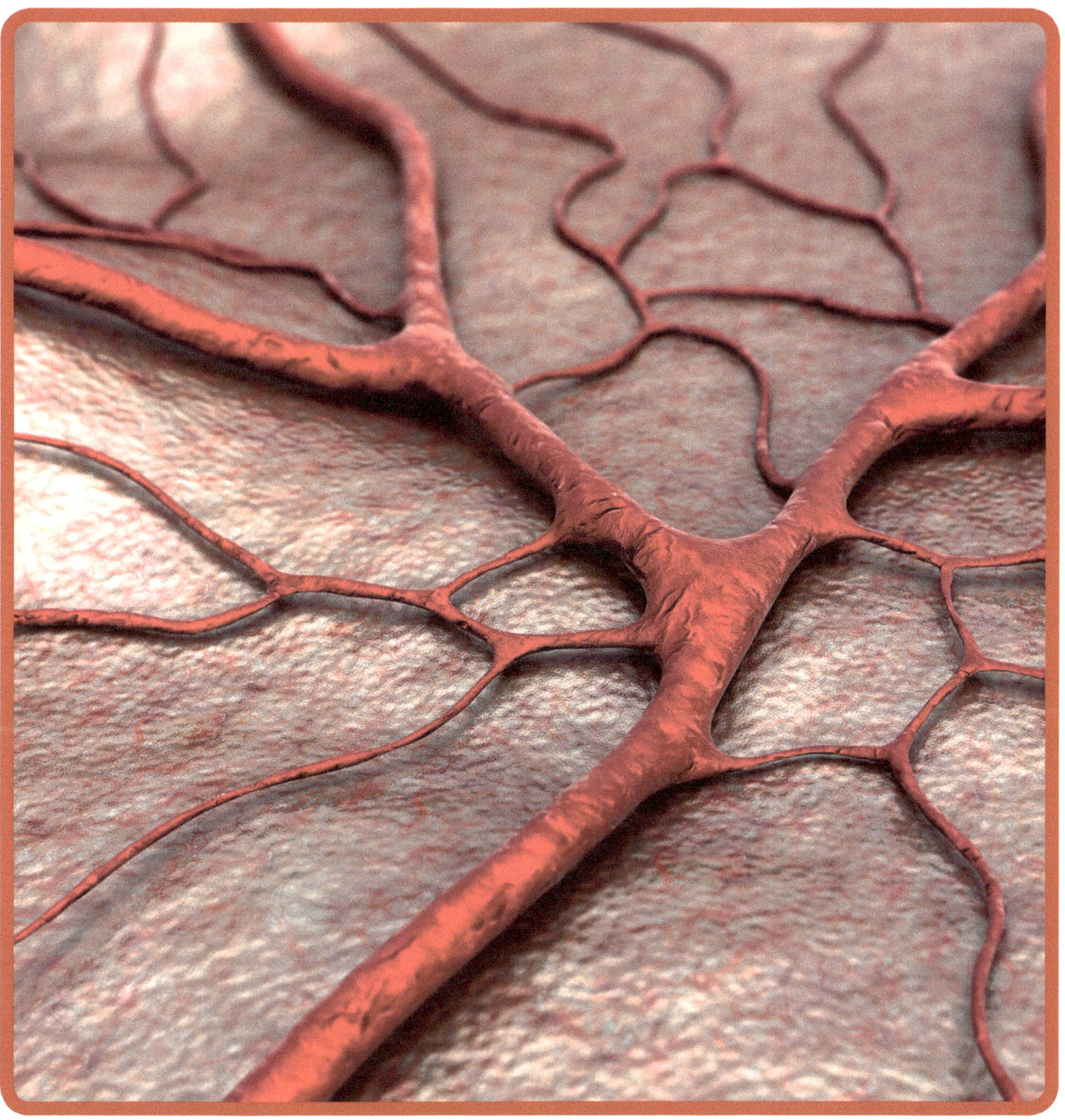

Veins are blood vessels
that carry blood
toward the heart.

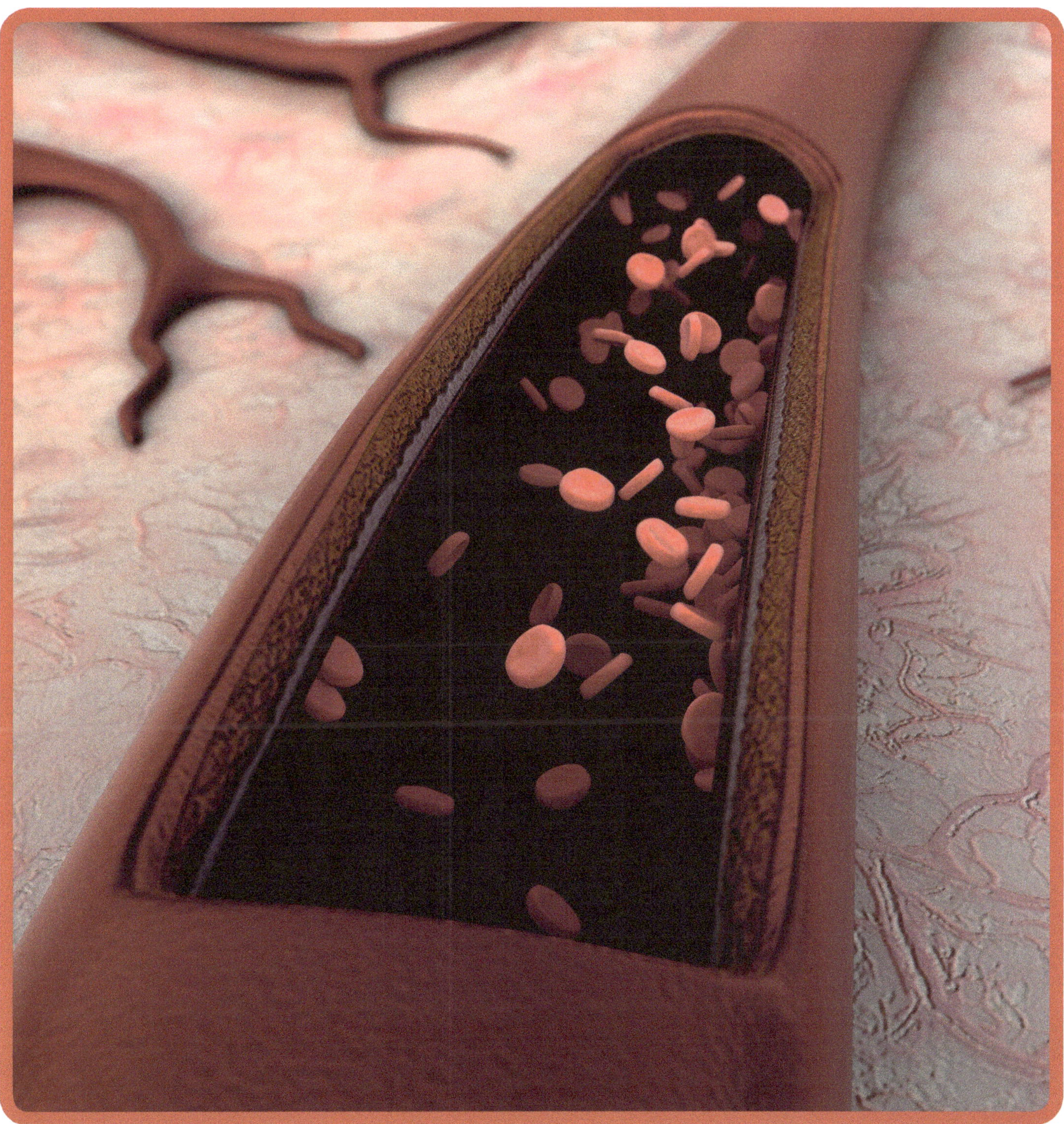

Most veins carry deoxygenated blood from the tissues back to the heart.

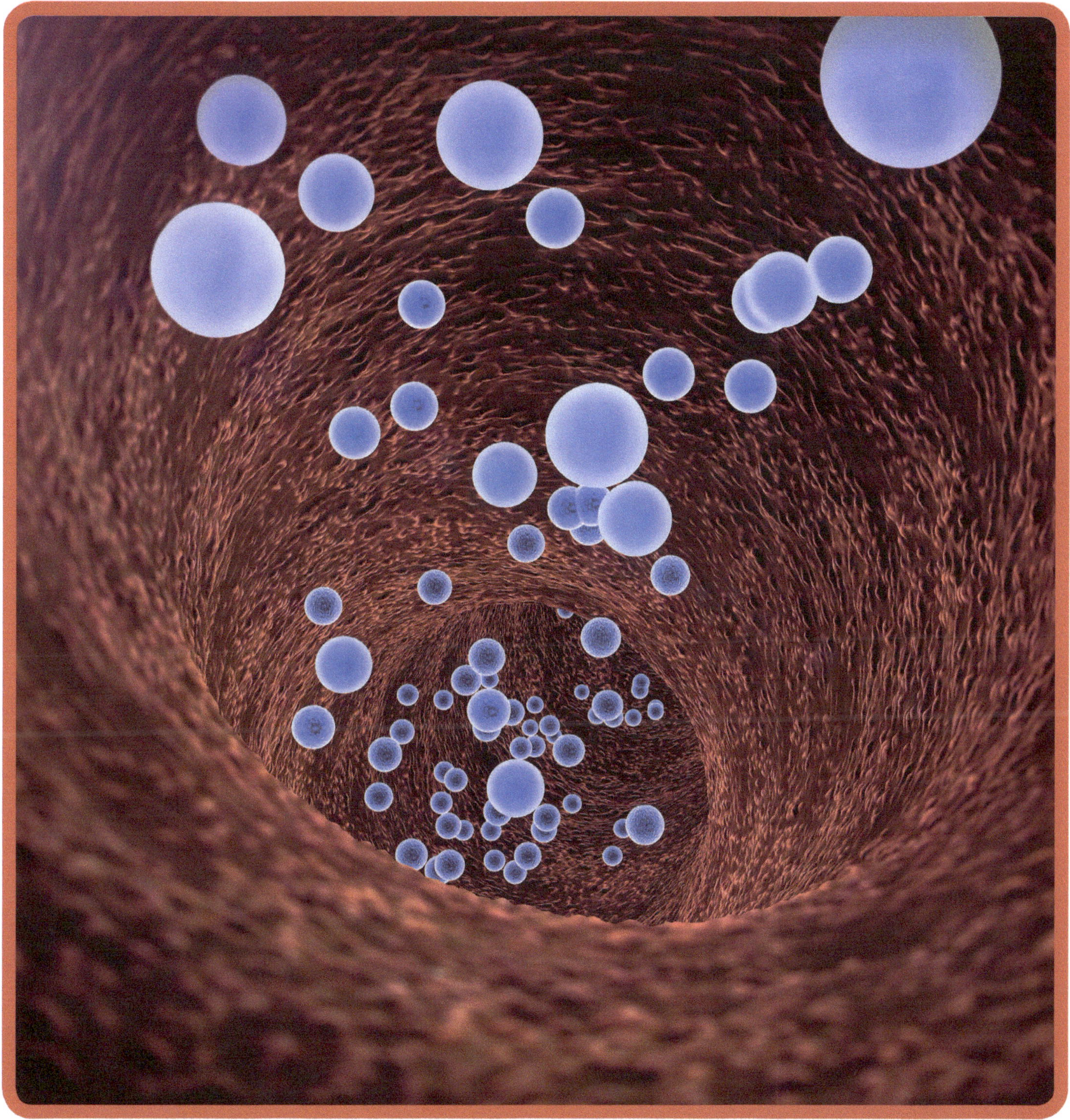

Veins are less muscular than arteries and are often closer to the skin.

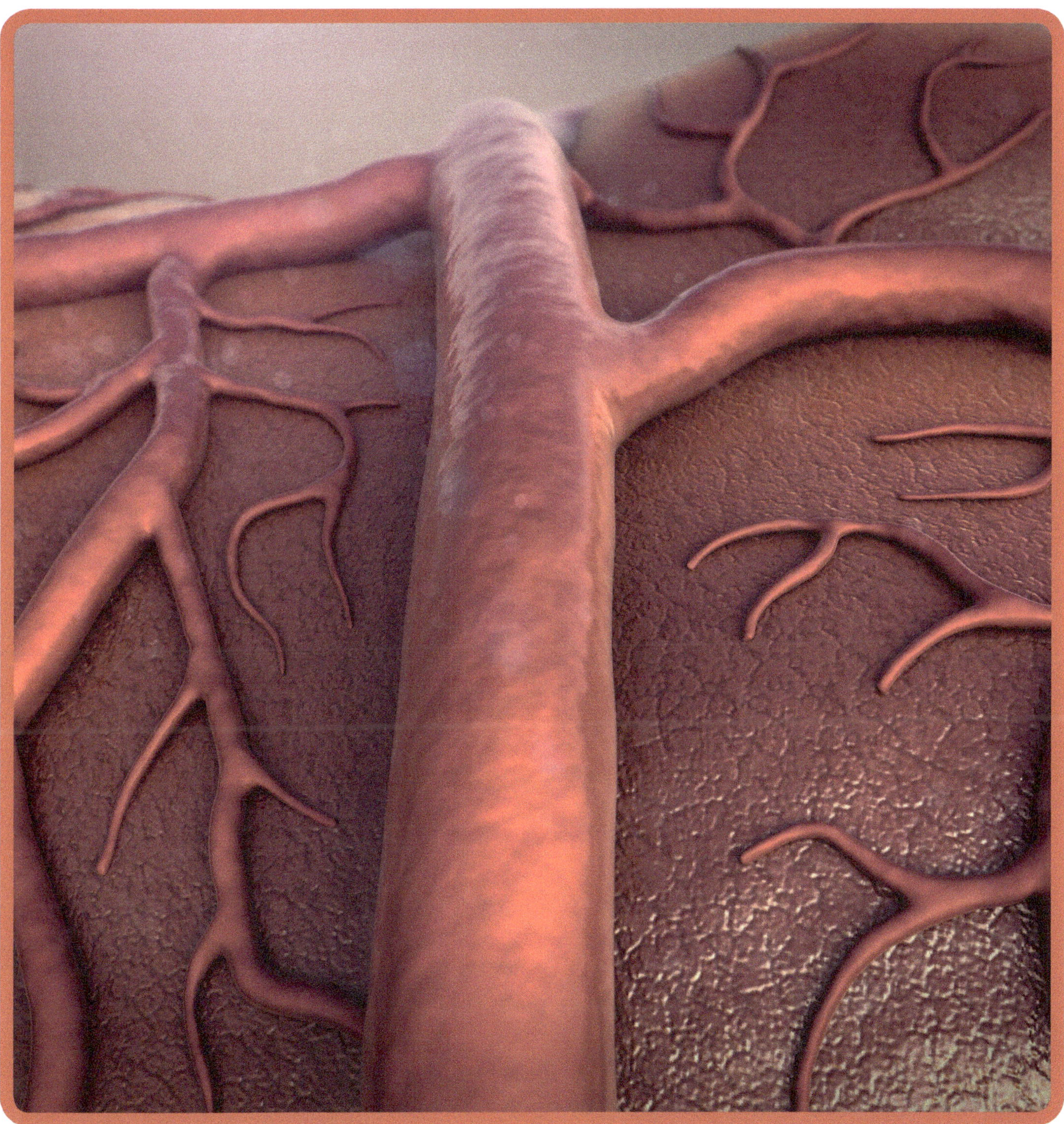

Coronary circulation is
the circulation of blood
in the blood vessels
of the heart muscle.

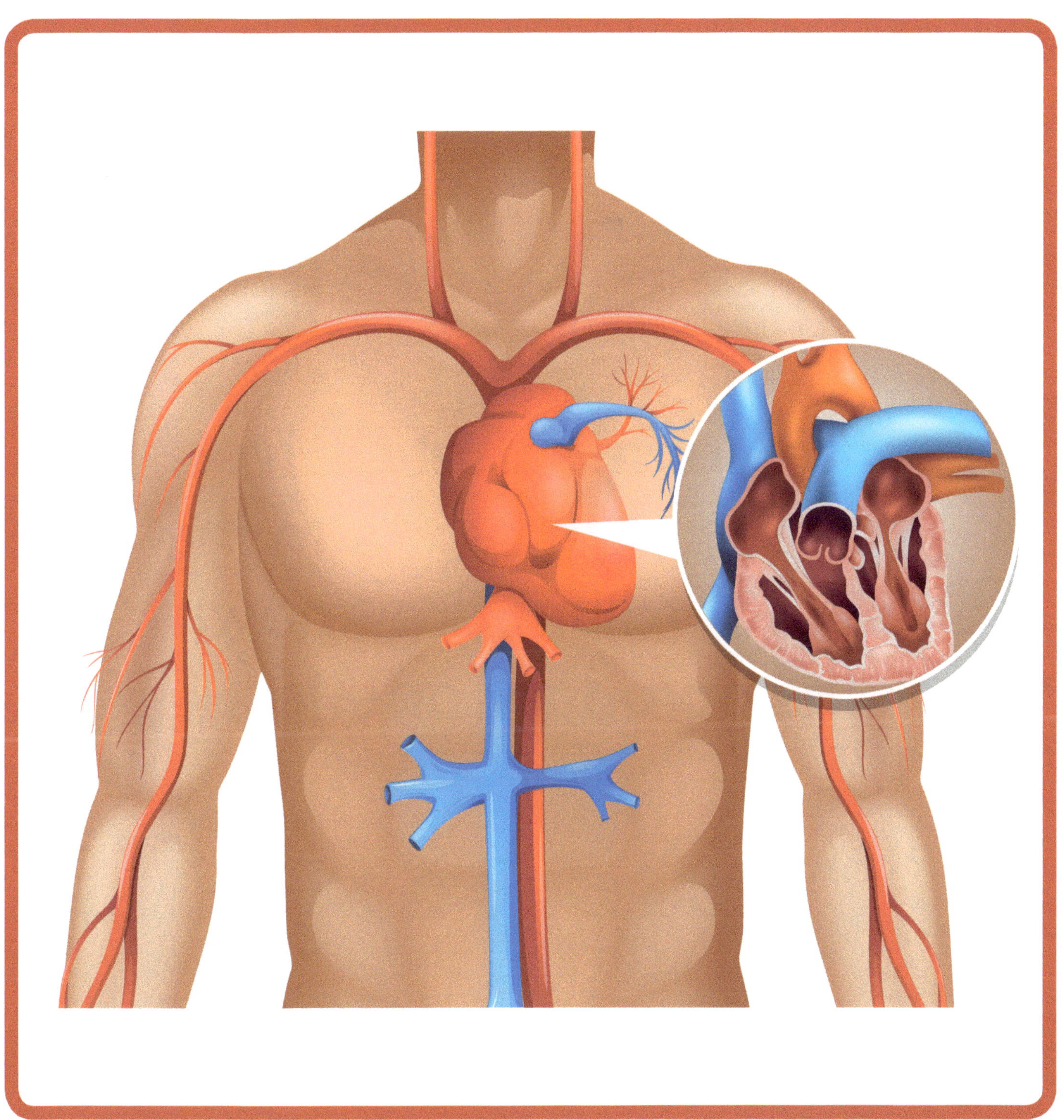

The vessels that deliver oxygen-rich blood to the myocardium are known as coronary arteries.

The vessels that remove the deoxygenated blood from the heart muscle are known as cardiac veins.

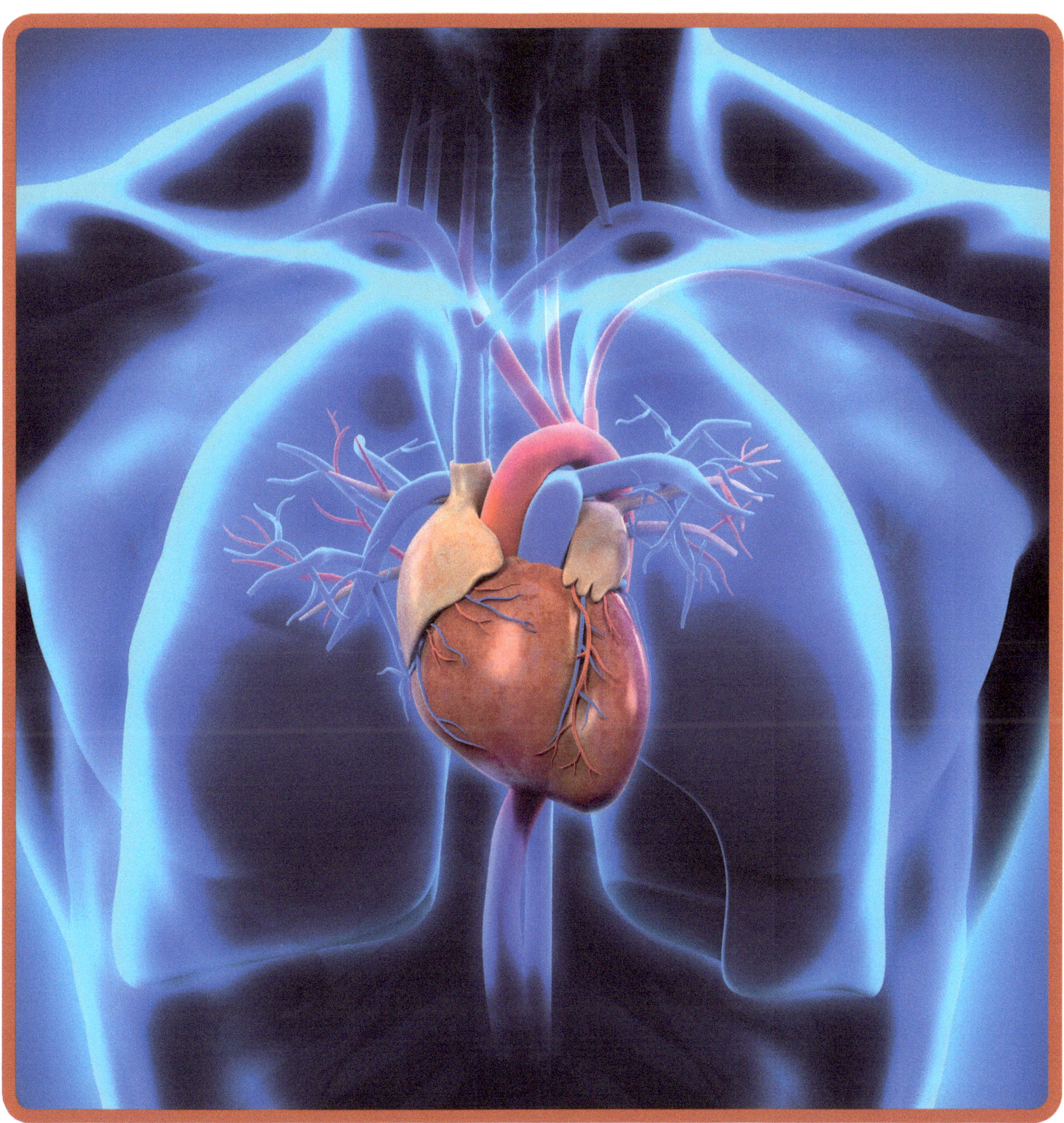

Human blood is colourless, it is the hemoglobin that makes it red.

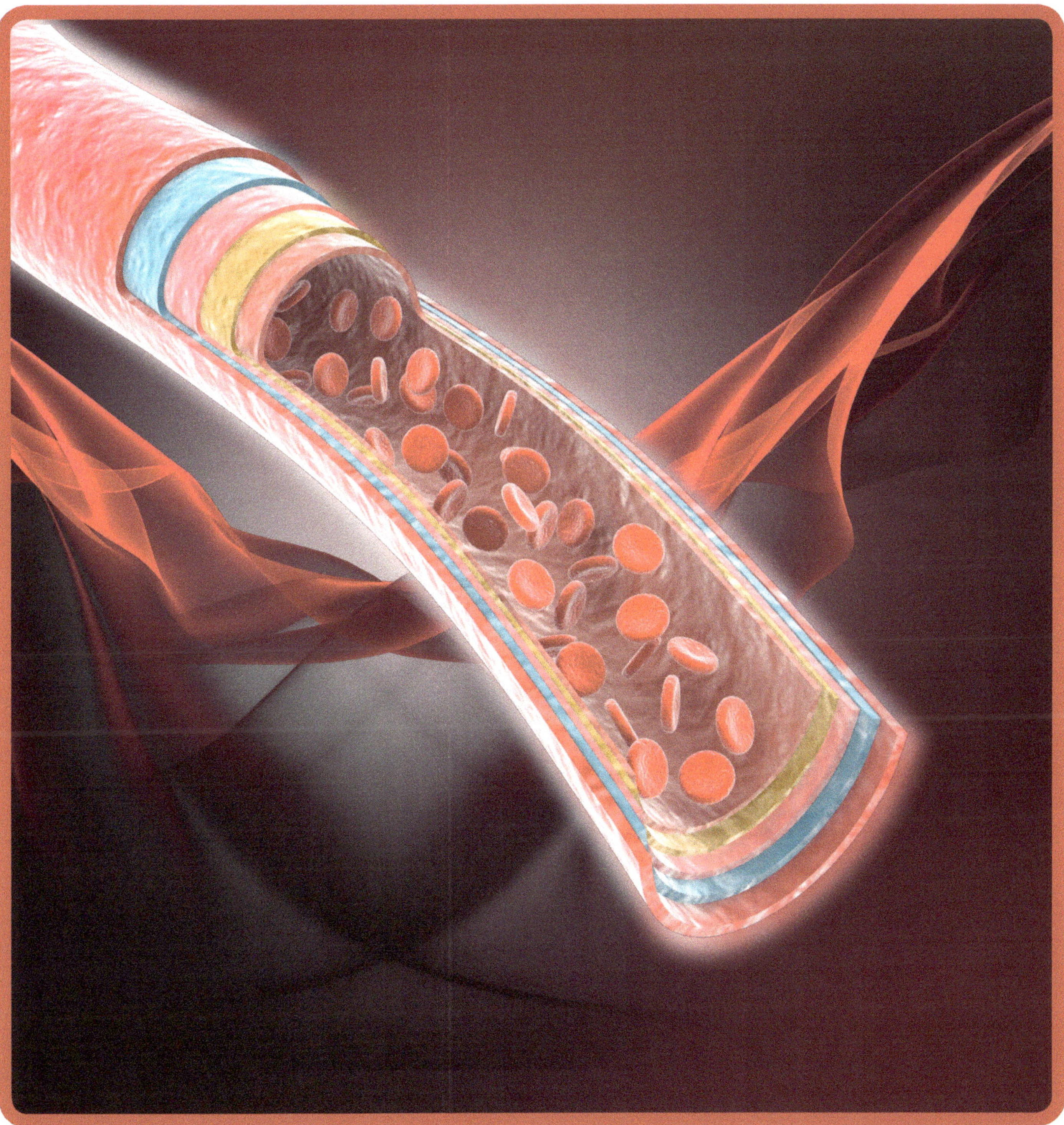

It takes 20 seconds
for blood to circulate
the entire body.
Oxygenated blood
leaves the aorta about
about 1 mile an hour.

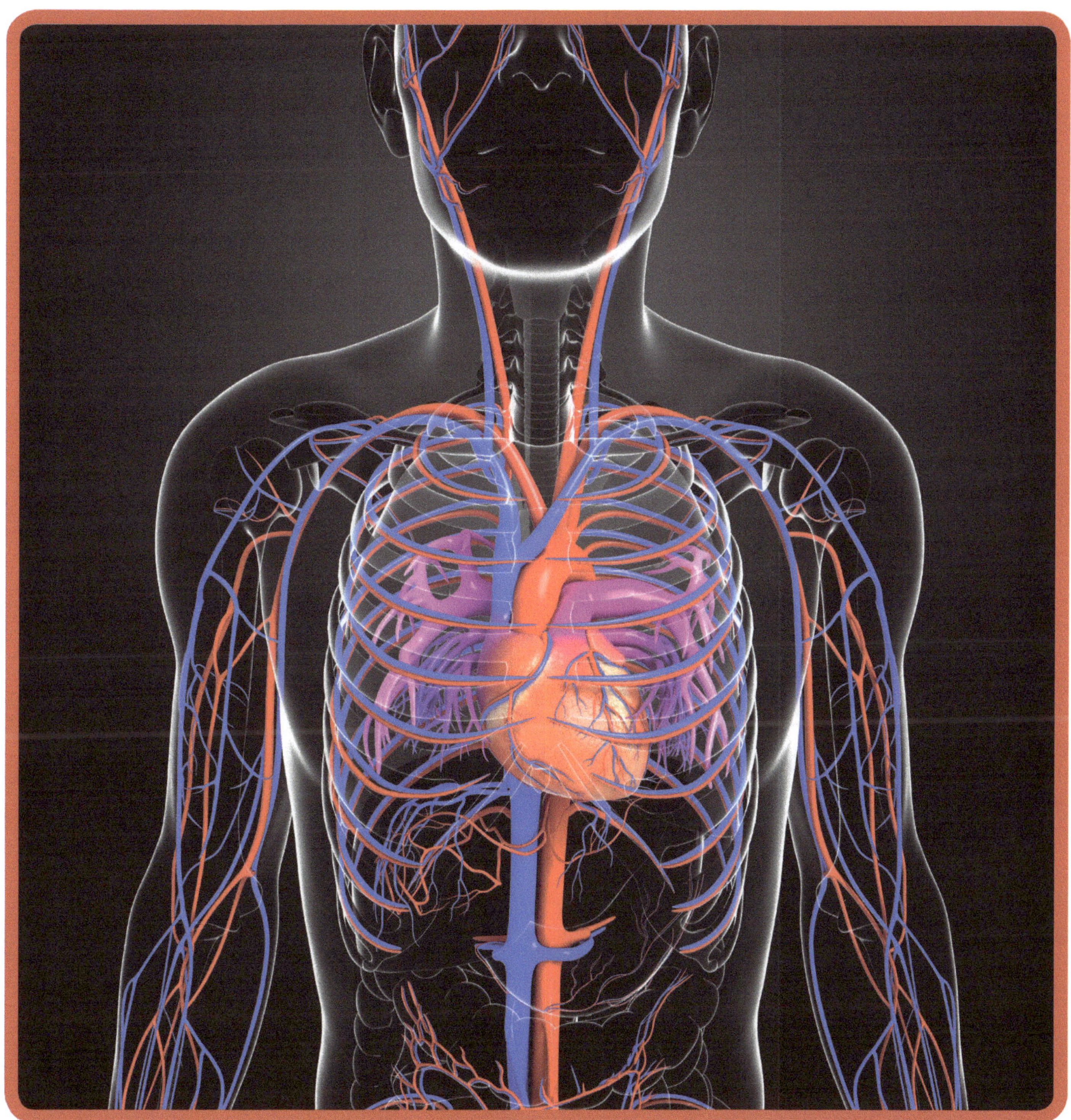

The heart contracts
tirelessly – more
than 2.5 billion times
over an average
lifetime – to pump blood
around the body.

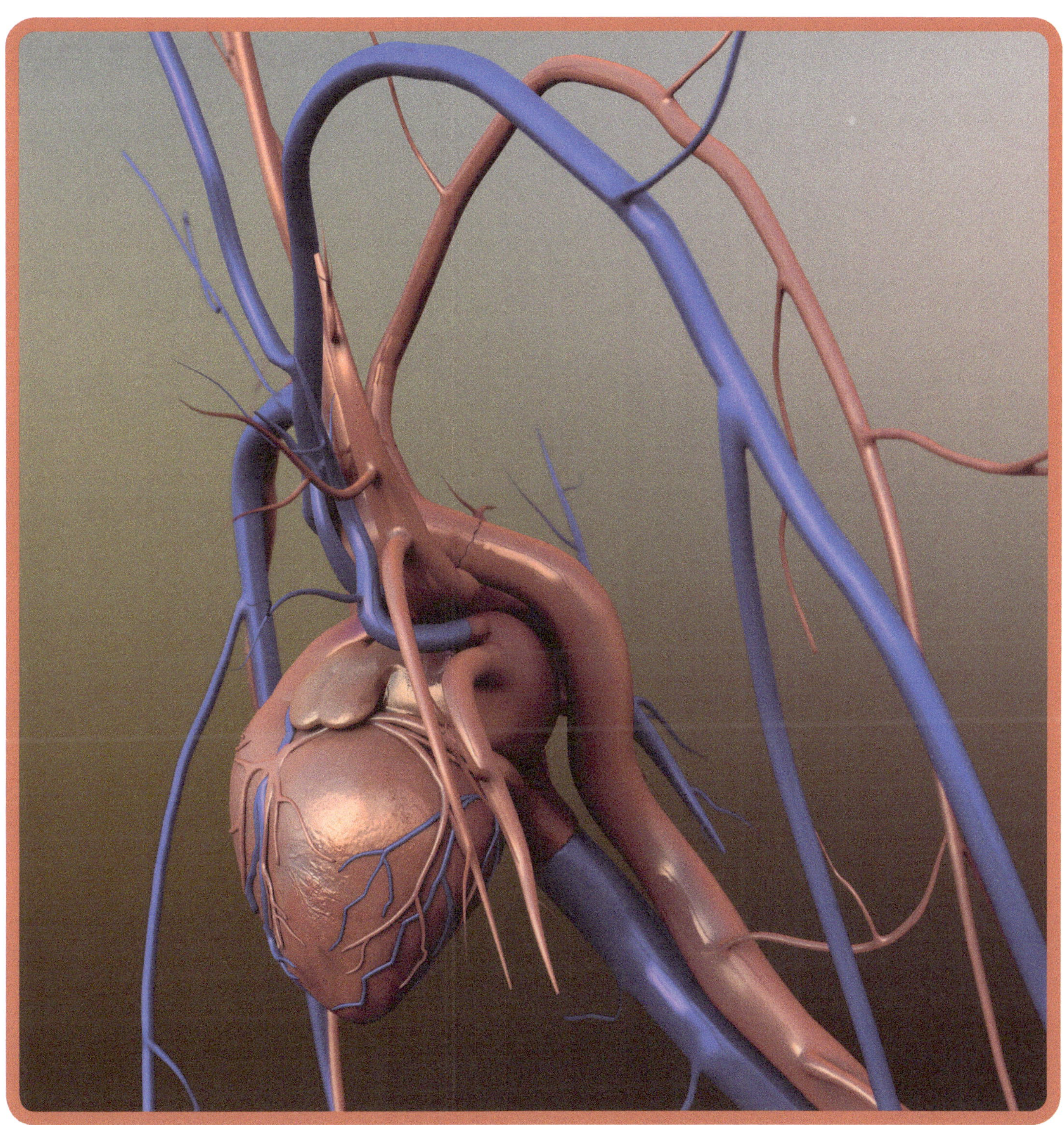

Visit

BABY PROFESSOR
EDUCATION KIDS

www.BabyProfessorBooks.com
to download Free Baby Professor eBooks
and view our catalog of new and exciting
Children's Books